# Goods and Services

by Mary Lindeen

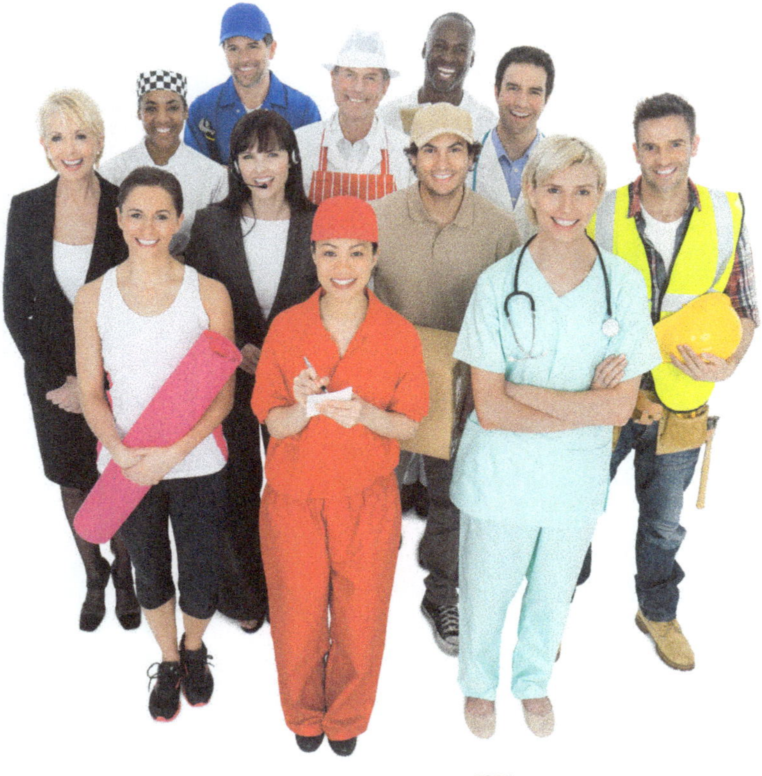

NORWOODHOUSE PRESS

Norwood House Press
Chicago, Illinois
For more information about Norwood House Press please visit our website at
www.norwoodhousepress.com or call 866-565-2900.
© 2020 Norwood House Press. Beginning-to-Read™ is a trademark of Norwood House Press.
All rights reserved. No part of this book may be reproduced or utilized in any form or by any means without written permission from the publisher.

Editor: Judy Kentor Schmauss
Designer: Sara Radka


**Photo Credits:**
Alamy, 15; Getty Images, cover, 1–10, 12–13, 16–29; Shutterstock, 11


**Library of Congress Cataloging-in-Publication Data**
Names: Lindeen, Mary, author.
Title: Goods and services / by Mary Lindeen.
Description: Chicago, Illinois : Norwood House Press, [2020] |
    Series: A beginning-to-read book | Audience: 5-8. | Audience: K to 3.
Identifiers: LCCN 2018054644 | ISBN 9781684509362 (hardcover) |
    ISBN 9781684044320 (pbk.) | ISBN 9781684044375 (ebook)
Subjects: LCSH: Commerce–Juvenile literature. | Consumption (Economics)–Juvenile literature.
Classification: LCC HF5392 .L56 2020 | DDC 381–dc23
LC record available at https://lccn.loc.gov/2018054644


Hardcover ISBN: 978-1-68450-936-2
Paperback ISBN: 978-1-68404-432-0

319N—072019
Manufactured in the United States of America in North Mankato, Minnesota.

Look at these apples.
They look delicious!

Apples are
good to eat.

Apples are
also **goods**.

Goods are things
people have
that were made
or grown.

This factory
makes crayons.

Crayons are
goods.

Clothes, toys,
bikes, and books
are goods, too.

Some goods are made or grown close to where we live.

Other goods come from far away.

Planes, trains, ships, and
trucks help deliver goods.

So can you!

This driver is delivering goods to a store.

Then people can go inside and buy them.

FA2550
YOUR M&S
OD

Overload Permit
5

Driving a truck is a **service**.

Services are jobs people do that help others.

A truck driver helps move goods from place to place.

Teaching is a
service, too.

A teacher helps
you learn.

Sometimes people pay for goods.

And sometimes they don't.

Sometimes people pay for services.

And sometimes they don't.

Some goods are things we need.

And some goods are things we want.

Some services give us help we need.

And some services give us help we want.

**Everyone**
uses goods
and services.

And everyone
can offer goods
and services to
others, too!

# . . . READING REINFORCEMENT . . .

## CRAFT AND STRUCTURE

To check your child's understanding of this book, recreate the following webs on a sheet of paper. Read the book with your child. For the web on the left, help your child fill in the circles with what he or she learned about goods. Do the same thing with your child for the web on the right about services.

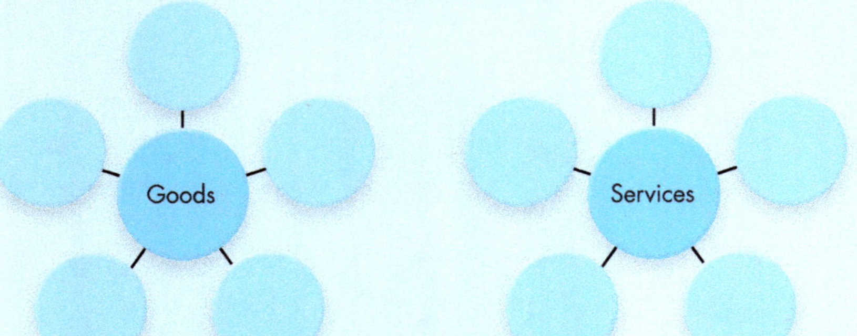

## VOCABULARY: Learning Content Words

Content words are words that are specific to a particular topic. All of the content words in this book can be found on page 32. Use some or all of these content words to complete one or more of the following activities:

- Choose a vocabulary word. Give your child several hints about the word's meaning and have him or her guess the word. Then have your child use the word in a sentence.

- Ask your child to draw pictures that will remind him or her of the words' meanings. Hold up a picture at random and ask your child which word the picture defines.

- Ask questions about the words that begin with *Who, What, Where, When, Why,* and *How.*

- Help your child with word associations, i.e., *What are two words that go together? Why? What are two words that are opposites?,* etc.

- Write the words on scraps of paper and place them in a bowl. Have your child pick one out of the bowl, say the word, its definition, and then use it in a sentence.

## FOUNDATIONAL SKILLS: Verbs

Verbs are action words. Have your child identify the words that are verbs in the list below. Then help your child find verbs in this book.

| | | | |
|---|---|---|---|
| car | write | sing | window |
| talk | trot | paper | speak |
| skip | saves | goes | flame |

## CLOSE READING OF INFORMATIONAL TEXT

Close reading helps children comprehend text. It includes reading a text, discussing it with others, and answering questions about it. Use these questions to discuss this book with your child:

- What's the difference between a good and a service?

- Are services wants or needs? Can they be both? How?

- What's an example of a service that is NOT in this book? Why is it a service?

- How does a grocery store provide goods and services?

- Are goods or services more important to you? Why?

- Can you have goods without services? How? Can you have services without goods? How?

## FLUENCY

Fluency is the ability to read accurately with speed and expression. Help your child practice fluency by using one or more of the following activities:

- Reread the book to your child at least two times while he or she uses a finger to track each word as it is read.

- Read a line of the book, then reread it as your child reads along with you.

- Ask your child to go back through the book and read the words he or she knows.

- Have your child practice reading the book several times to improve accuracy, rate, and expression.

*Goods and Services* uses the 77 words listed below. *High-frequency words* are those words that are used most often in the English language. They are sometimes referred to as sight words because children need to learn to recognize them automatically when they read. *Content words* are any words specific to a particular topic. Regular practice reading these words will enhance your child's ability to read with greater fluency and comprehension.

## High-Frequency Words

| | | | | |
|---|---|---|---|---|
| a | eat | look | that | us |
| also | for | made | them | uses |
| and | from | make(s) | then | want |
| are | give | or | these | we |
| at | go | other(s) | they | were |
| away | good(s) | people | things | where |
| can | have | place | this | you |
| come | help(s) | so | to | |
| do | is | some | too | |

## Content Words

| | | | | |
|---|---|---|---|---|
| apples | delicious | far | need | store |
| bikes | deliver(ing) | grown | offer | teacher |
| books | don't | inside | pay | teaching |
| buy | driver | jobs | planes | toys |
| close | driving | learn | service(s) | trains |
| clothes | everyone | live | ships | truck(s) |
| crayons | factory | move | sometimes | |

### ••• About the Author

Mary Lindeen is a writer, editor, parent, and former elementary school teacher. She has written more than 100 books for children and edited many more. She specializes in early literacy instruction and books for young readers, especially nonfiction.